STEP-UP SCIENCE

Moving and Growing

Louise and Richard Spilsbury

Evans

Published by Evans Brothers Limited
2A Portman Mansions
Chiltern Street
London W1U 6NR

© Evans Brothers Limited 2007

Produced for Evans Brothers Limited by
White-Thomson Publishing Ltd,
Bridgewater Business Centre,
210 High Street,
Lewes, East Sussex BN7 2NH

Printed in China by by New Era Printing Co. Ltd

Project manager: Rachel Minay

Designer: Flick, Book Design and Graphics

Consultant: Jackie Holderness,
Educational Consultant and Writer

British Library Cataloguing in Publication Data

Moving and growing. – (Step-up science)

   1. Animal mechanics – Juvenile literature
   2. Growth – Juvenile literature
   3. Animal locomotion – Juvenile literature
   591.4'79

ISBN-13: 9780237532079
ISBN-10: 0237532077

Acknowledgements:

The authors would like to thank Scott Fisher,
teacher at Stokenham Area Primary School for his
invaluable comments and advice on this series.

Picture acknowledgements:

Martyn f. Chillmaid: pages 11t, 13r. CORBIS: pages
4t (Paul Barton), 7r (Lester V. Bergman), 23b, 25,
26t (Tom Stewart). Istockphoto: cover (top left and
right), title page, pages 4b, 5, 6–7, 11b, 14, 15r,
17b, 17 inset tl, 17 inset tc, 17 inset tr, 17 inset bl,
17 inset bc, 17 inset br, 18t, 19tl, 19 tc, 19b, 20,
26b, 24, 28b, 29. NHPA/Photoshot: cover (main)
(Andy Rouse), pages 15b (George Bernard), 16r
(James Carmichael Jr), 17t (Martin Harvey), 18b
(Andy Rouse). Nicholas, Bella: page 19tr.
OSF/Photolibrary: pages 15c, 8 (Dynamic Graphics
[UK] Ltd), 15t (David M. Dennis), 16l (Rodger
Jackman), 21 (Index Stock Imagery), 22 (Mauritius
Die Bildagentur Gmbh), 23t (Bsip). Science Photo
Library: page 9 (Sovereign, ISM); TopFoto: page 27
(ImageWorks).

Illustrations by Ian Thompson (pages 10, 12, 13l).

Contents

Moving and growing

Humans and other animals can move and grow. We can classify or divide all living things by these two features. All living things can move by themselves without outside help. All living things are also able to grow. From the beginning of its life, a living thing uses food to provide the energy its body needs to grow bigger. Non-living things only move when pushed or pulled by something else. An example of this is when a ball is kicked or a flag is blown by the wind.

How do we know that the people and plants in this picture are living things but that the ball is a non-living thing? ▶

On the move

People and animals need to move to find food. They also move to find partners in order to reproduce and have young. Many animals need to move to escape danger. Living things move in different ways. Plants may not appear to move because they are rooted to one place, but plants move as they grow and get taller. Some plants have leaves and flowers that turn to face the sunlight.

Living things

Seven life processes classify plants and animals as living things:

Movement Animals move from place to place. Plants move leaves to catch sunlight.

Respiration Respiration is how animals and plants turn their food into energy.

Sensitivity Living things are sensitive to, or aware of, their surroundings and can respond to them.

Growth Baby animals become adults. New plants become larger plants.

Bones

Many animals and all humans have hard, white bones inside their bodies. These bones form the skeleton that makes the framework of the body and helps the body to move. As the human or animal grows, the bones of its skeleton grow with it. Bones grow steadily throughout childhood. This is why children outgrow clothes and shoes so quickly.

We cannot see our bones easily because they are inside us. However, if you make a tight fist, you can see and feel the hard, strong knucklebones at the base of each finger.

Reproduction All living things have young.

Excretion Living things excrete, or get rid of, their body's waste products.

Nutrition Plants make their own food. Animals eat plants or other animals.

MRS GREN is a mnemonic, a word made from the first letters of the seven features above to help us remember them. Can you make up a mnemonic of your own?

Marie Curie

X-ray photos show the bones inside the body. Marie Curie was a scientist whose studies were vital in developing the use of X-rays in surgery. Look up her name on a search engine and find out how her work helped to develop X-rays.

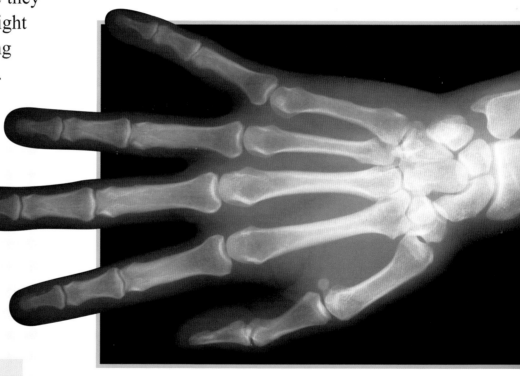

▲ *X-rays can pass through clothes and flesh but not hard bone. An X-ray photo can show the bones inside a body as white shapes. The human hand has 27 bones. How many of these can you actually feel inside your hand?*

A frame of bones

The human skeleton is the framework for the body. The skeleton gives us our shape.

Different bones

An adult's skeleton has over 200 bones that vary greatly in size and shape. The skull is hard and round. The skull is attached to the spine (backbone), at the neck. An adult's spine is made of 26 separate bones called vertebrae. Each vertebra is shaped like a ring. There are 12 pairs of ribs that form a sort of cage. All of the ribs are attached to the spine. The pelvis, which connects the spine to the legs, is butterfly-shaped.

The smallest bone in the human body is the stirrup bone inside the ear, which measures just 2.5 mm. The longest is the femur, or thigh bone, which is usually about a quarter of a person's height.

Make a skeleton

Look at the picture of the skeleton and think about the symmetry of the two sides of the body. Then make a skeleton for yourself. You could use white paper drinking straws to make a small skeleton or make thin rolls of newspaper and tape them together to make a large skeleton that can be hung up on a door.

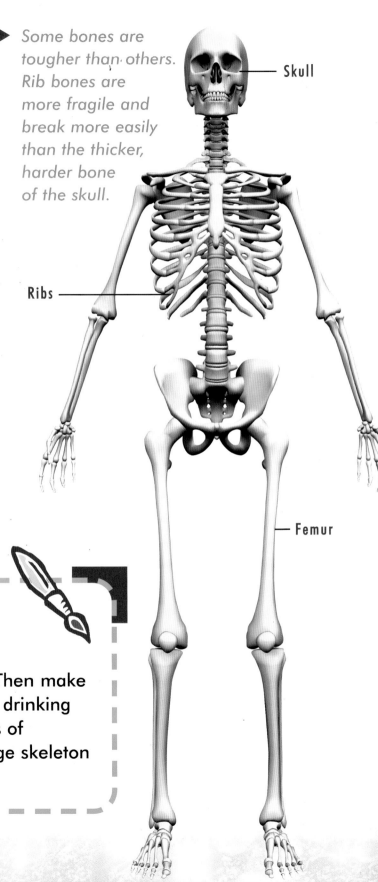

▶ Some bones are tougher than others. Rib bones are more fragile and break more easily than the thicker, harder bone of the skull.

Skull

Ribs

Femur

Strong but light

Bones are hard and strong so they can support the weight of a human body. As a material, bone is lighter than steel, but – for its weight – it is much stronger. Bones are hard on the outside but have hollow spaces inside, which makes them light, so people and animals do not weigh too much and can move around easily. In the centre of bones there is a soft spongy substance called bone marrow. The bone marrow makes new blood for the rest of the body.

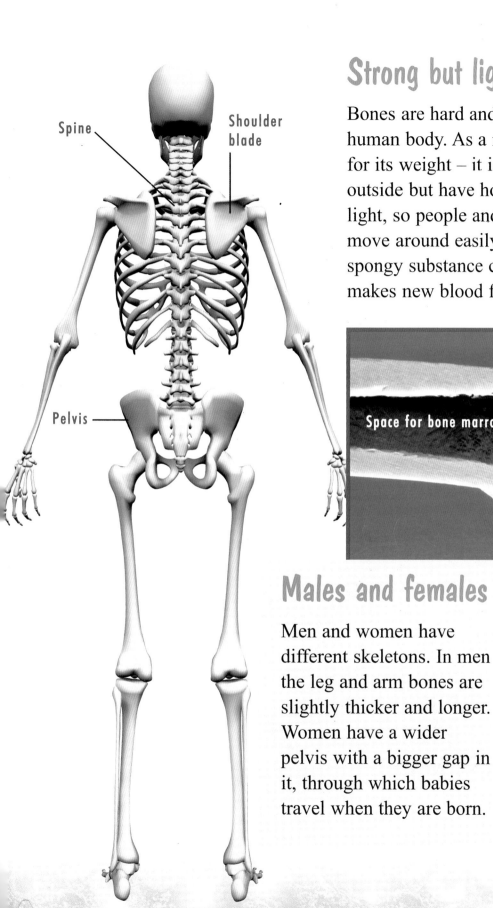

Spine

Shoulder blade

Pelvis

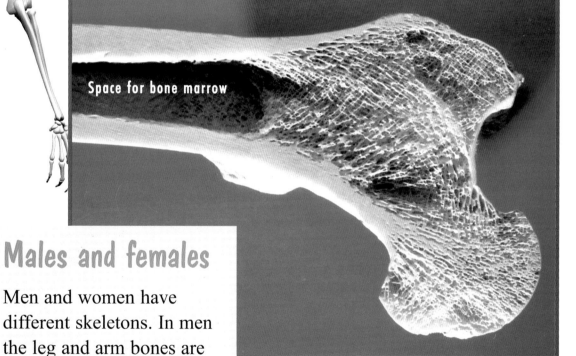

Space for bone marrow

Males and females

Men and women have different skeletons. In men the leg and arm bones are slightly thicker and longer. Women have a wider pelvis with a bigger gap in it, through which babies travel when they are born.

▲ This is a photo of the inside of a bone. We can see that the outer shell of the bone is solid, but the middle is mostly hollow. The bone marrow would have been in the hollow part of the bone.

Support and protection

The skeleton not only helps a human to move, it also provides support and protection. The skeleton is the structure that enables a human to stand up. Without bones, a human would just be a floppy pile of skin and body parts on the floor. Bones also protect the delicate organs inside the body.

Bones and structure

The bones that make up the skeleton support and give structure to the body in many ways. For example, bones support the skin, which covers the whole body. The spine holds the body and head erect, or upright, when a person is standing. The skull forms the framework for the head. It is made up of two sets of bones. The front set forms the forehead and the roof of the eye sockets, giving the face its distinctive shape.

Jelly men

Without a skeleton a human would be as floppy as a beanbag and as shapeless as a big blob of jelly. Draw people whose skeletons have suddenly disappeared!

▲ The spinal column forms the major part of the skeleton. It supports all the upper body parts when we stand up.

Shielding the organs

Many organs are soft and would be damaged if knocked. Bones provide a protective cover around these delicate parts. For example, the skull is a set of bones fused, or joined, together to protect the brain. The ribs protect the heart, which pumps blood around the body. They also protect the lungs, which allow us to breathe. The spine protects the spinal cord, a bundle of nerves that carries messages from the brain to the rest of the body.

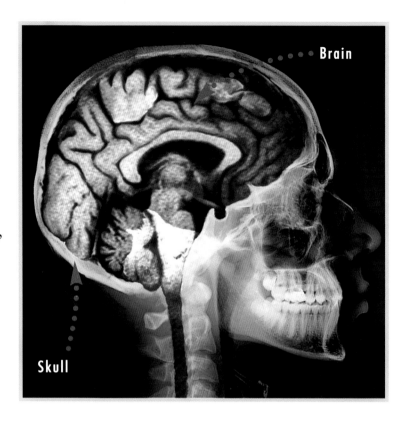

▶ *The brain is the body's control centre. It allows us to think, move, see, feel and hear. The brain is very soft and needs the skull to protect it.*

Concept map

A concept map shows the connections between different concepts, or ideas. This concept map shows the connections between bones and the body. Where would you put skin and muscles on this concept map and what would you say about them?

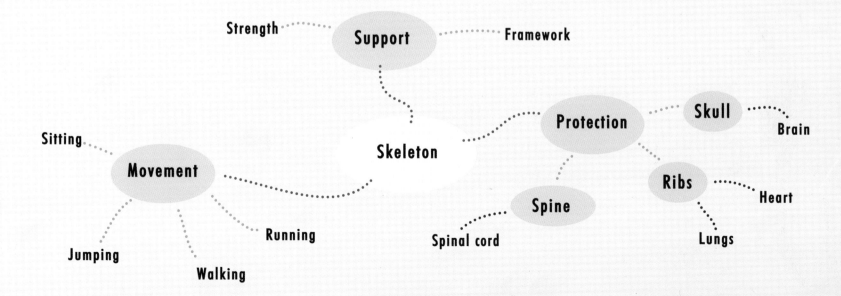

How bones move

Bones cannot move by themselves. Bones are attached to muscles and only move when muscles pull them. The muscles only work when we want them to. For example, when the brain sends a message through nerves to the muscles in the arm telling it to lift a ball or cup, those muscles pull the arm bones to make the arm work.

Muscles at work

Muscles contract when they pull, which means they get shorter and harder. Try holding your upper arm as you bend your lower arm up. You should be able to feel the upper arm muscle, or biceps muscle, bulge. It is contracting and pulling the bones in your lower arm upward.

Muscle pairs

Muscles can only pull; they cannot push. To make bones move backwards and forwards we need pairs of muscles. When one muscle contracts, the other relaxes, becoming long and thin again.

If you feel the underside of your upper arm when it is bent, you will notice that the triceps muscle feels soft and relaxed compared to the biceps on the upper side.

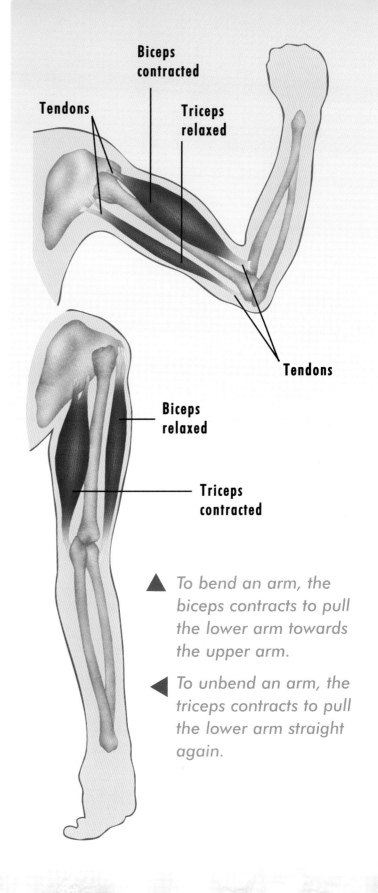

▲ To bend an arm, the biceps contracts to pull the lower arm towards the upper arm.

◀ To unbend an arm, the triceps contracts to pull the lower arm straight again.

If you now straighten your arm, you should be able to feel the biceps muscle relax and the triceps muscle bulge.

Tendons

Muscles are attached to the bones by tendons. Tendons are tough and cord-like and act a bit like thick elastic bands. They get tighter when a muscle contracts. Tendons help us make delicate movements such as wiggling our fingers or toes.

Tendons are very important to help us move. If the Achilles tendon is damaged, it is difficult or impossible to walk.

▲ When we smile and talk, muscles help us move our cheekbones and jawbones. It takes 32 muscles to frown but only 7 to smile, so say 'Cheese!'

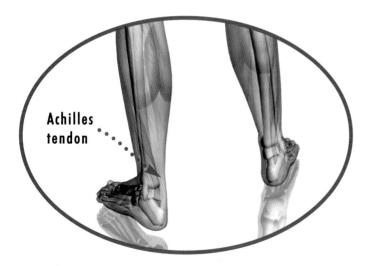

Achilles tendon

▲ Can you find and feel the Achilles tendon? It is like a rope between the back of your heel and your calf muscle at the back of your lower leg.

Make a moving arm!

Make a simple arm from card and move it using string muscles. Follow the instructions at http://www.channel4.com/learning/microsites/E/essentials/science/worksheets/4A_B.doc

Joints and bones

Joints are the places where bones meet. The individual bones of a skeleton are completely rigid, but joints connect bones to bones so that they can move. Different types of joint allow different kinds of movement throughout the body.

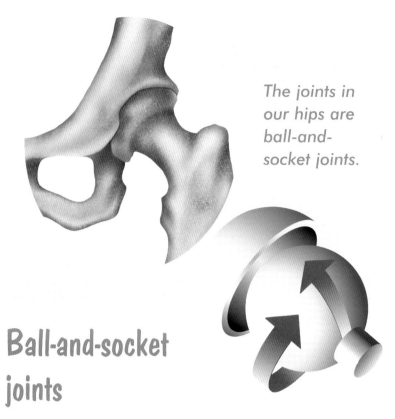

The joints in our hips are ball-and-socket joints.

The elbow joint is a kind of hinge joint.

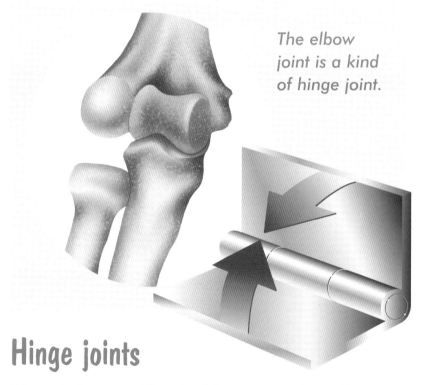

Hinge joints

These joints are like the hinges on a door. Just as most doors can only open one way, a hinge joint only bends in one direction. The knees have hinge joints, which let us bend and then straighten our legs. There are also many smaller hinge joints in the fingers and toes.

Ball-and-socket joints

Ball-and-socket joints are found at the shoulders and hips. In this type of joint, one bone has a rounded end, shaped like a ball, which sits inside a small cup-shaped area at the end of another bone. Ball-and-socket joints allow for lots of movement in every direction. Find an open space and try swinging your arms all around to feel just how much movement the ball-and-socket joint gives you!

Ligaments

The bones at a joint are held together by ligaments. These are thick bands of stretchy tissue that act like elastic bands, holding the bones in place as well as allowing them to move.

Sliding joints

Sliding joints are found between the surfaces of two flat bones. There are sliding joints in the spine. The vertebrae in the spine have discs, or pads, of cartilage between them.

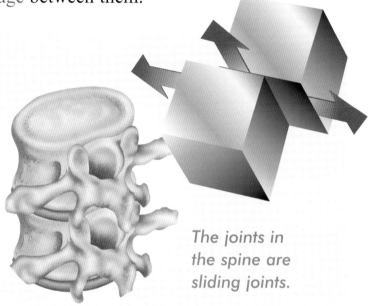

The joints in the spine are sliding joints.

▲ The bones in the spine are closely linked but move across each other at the joints so we can bend. The distance between this girl's fingertips and the floor is being measured to see how flexible her spine is.

Cartilage is smooth and flexible and the bones slide slightly over these pads. Because it is made of so many vertebrae bones, with cartilage discs between, the spine is very flexible. It can bend and twist in many different directions.

How do you think the discs of cartilage also help long-jumpers when they land on the ground with a thud after a jump?

Jumping joints

Make a skeleton move at three different joints at http://insideout.rigb.org/ri/anatomy/casing_the_joint/joints_explorer.html. Click on each joint to learn more about it.

Animal skeletons

Humans and other animals with bony skeletons are classified as vertebrates. Fish, amphibians (such as toads and frogs), reptiles (such as snakes and lizards), birds and mammals are all vertebrates.

The same but different

All vertebrates have a spine made up of lots of vertebrae linked together and a skull. Most also have four limbs, which connect to the shoulder and pelvis bones. In humans, the limbs are arms and legs with hands and feet. In many animals, the limbs are four legs with paws, as in cats and dogs. However, in birds, limbs take the form of wings. In fish, the limbs are fins, which help the fish to swim.

Big and small

Large animals, such as rhinoceroses or elephants, have big, heavy bones because their bodies are also big and heavy and they need the extra support. Many smaller animals, such as fish and chickens, have smaller, thinner and therefore weaker bones. Some, such as the Humboldt penguin, which dives in the sea to catch fish, have relatively heavy bones to help weigh them down in the water. Young or small pets, such as kittens or mice, have very delicate bones, which is why we should handle them carefully and gently at all times.

▲ Did you know giraffes and humans have the same number of bones in their necks? However, a giraffe's vertebrae are much, much longer!

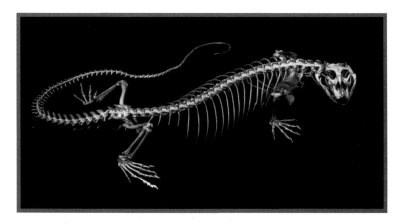

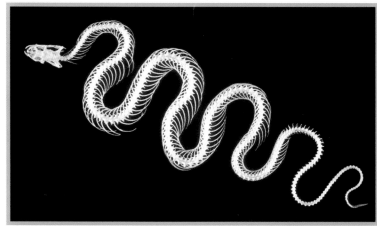

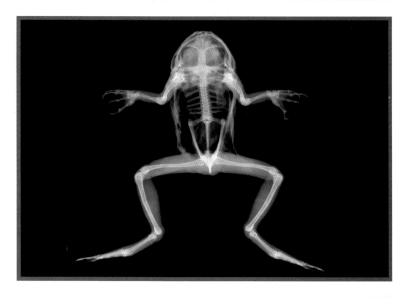

Fossils

We know about dinosaurs and other vertebrates that died millions of years ago because of bone fossils. Their soft body parts were the first things to rot away, leaving the bones. The bones gradually became buried by mud or sand, which turned to stone around them. The bones rotted and left their shape in the stone. Different stone then formed in the shape left behind, making fossils the same shape as the original bones.

Which fossils could you recognise? Do you think it is important to study animals that lived long ago? Why?

Dino bones

It is hard to rebuild animal skeletons from fossil bones when many are broken up or lost. It's like putting together a jigsaw with missing pieces!

You can have fun putting together a dinosaur's bones at http://www.bbc.co.uk/sn/prehistoric_life/games/skeleton_jigsaw

Animals without bones

More than nine out of every ten animals in the world is an invertebrate, an animal that does not have a bony skeleton. Invertebrates include insects, crabs, jellyfish, spiders and snails. Nearly all animal bodies need support and protection but how do invertebrates get theirs?

Exoskeletons

Some invertebrates have a protective layer, like an armoured box, outside the body. This is called an exoskeleton. It is strong and waterproof and it protects and supports the soft inner body. Insects such as beetles have exoskeletons made of a plastic-like substance called chitin. Crabs and snails have tough shells made of calcium carbonate, or chalk.

▲ A millipede is very flexible because of the many segments in its exoskeleton.

◀ A lobster's tough exoskeleton protects it against attack by hungry **predators**.

How invertebrates grow

An invertebrate with an exoskeleton has a problem. As it grows, the exoskeleton gets too small. Many invertebrates, including beetles, have to shed their exoskeletons when their bodies become too big. Underneath, the invertebrate has a new exoskeleton that hardens when the old one falls away. Some invertebrates cannot grow a bigger shell. The hermit crab has to take over a larger empty shell when its old one gets too small.

*In order to grow, a cockroach must regularly **moult**, or shed its skin.*

Liquid-filled bodies

Other invertebrates, such as earthworms, jellyfish and slugs, have soft outer bodies. They have no hard exoskeleton to give them shape and support. Instead, their bodies are packed with liquid – mostly water – that keeps them stiff, just as a water balloon becomes firm when it is filled with water.

Sea slugs are invertebrates with liquid-filled bodies.

Groups

Classify (divide) this set of animals into two groups: vertebrates and invertebrates.

How do animals move?

All animals need to move in ways suited to their habitat. They evolve skeleton shapes that help them move quickly to find or catch food or to escape danger. Although vertebrates move in very different ways, they are still using the same parts – muscles, joints, tendons and bones.

Animals on land

In a rainforest, gibbons have arms that are more than twice the length of their bodies and extra long fingers and toes that they use to swing between branches. In a desert, snakes move by curving their flexible skeletons and then pushing against the sand to move forwards. A kangaroo has long back feet and legs to push off the ground so it can leap across wide grassy spaces in Australia.

▼ *The cheetah is the fastest animal on land. Its flexible spine and long legs help it take long strides as it runs.*

fly slither

glide gallop stalk hover coil prance

prowl canter wiggle soar

slink trot leap slide

▲ Can you match four of these verbs, which describe kinds of movement, to the animals in these pictures? For example, horses trot and canter. How else do they move?

◀ A fish's fin bones help it steer through the water. Its tail acts like a propeller to move the fish along.

Animals in water

Fish have long flexible spines that help them move from side to side to swim. Unlike fish, whales and dolphins have flippers, which they use to steer themselves. They swim by moving their tails up and down. Penguins cannot fly but their stiff, flat wings are used for swimming instead.

Shape poem

This is a shape poem, written in the shape of a snail and it describes how a snail moves. Write a shape poem of your own about the way an animal moves and try to use as many adjectives as you can.

The snail's stomach muscles pull it slowly over the slimy slippery trail it secretes as it slides along.

Growth

▼ A baby is born with about 300 bones. As bones grow, some fuse together. A fully grown adult has only 206 bones.

When a vertebrate is born, its skeleton is much smaller than its mother's. As animals and humans grow older, their bones grow longer and bigger, so they become taller and heavier.

People reach adulthood, or maturity, at the age of about 20. This is when their bones stop lengthening and they stop growing in height.

Changing bones

A vertebrate's bones begin to develop as it grows inside its mother. The skeleton of a newborn baby is made of cartilage. As he or she grows, most of this cartilage becomes hard bone, except in places such as the tip of the nose and the ears, where it remains flexible.

A baby's skull is almost the same size as it will be when the baby has grown into an adult. At birth, the bones that make up the cranium, or back of the head, are not fused together. This means the skull can be flexible when the baby squeezes through the mother's birth canal. The separate sections of bone join together into solid bone by the time a child is about two years old.

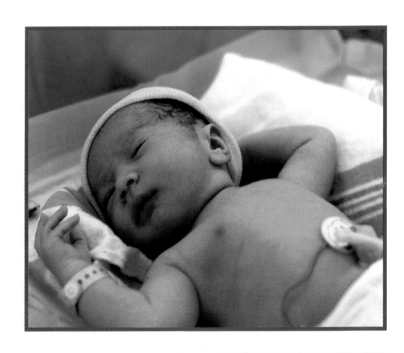

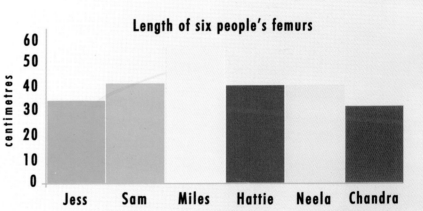

Length of six people's femurs

centimetres: 60, 50, 40, 30, 20, 10, 0

Jess — Sam — Miles — Hattie — Neela — Chandra

The length of a person's femur and their height are related. Miles is the tallest. Who is likely to be the shortest?

Growing bones

The human body is made up of millions of tiny cells. These cells are so small they can only be seen through a powerful microscope. Bones are a mix of hard substances and living cells. Like other cells in the body, blood brings bone cells food and oxygen to keep them alive. Bone cells can then increase in number to make bones gradually grow longer.

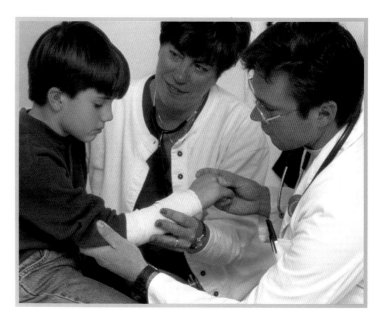

▲ When someone breaks a bone, it needs to be held rigid until the bone can heal itself. Broken bones are usually held in place by splints like this. This ensures the bone heals quickly and in the correct shape.

Investigating head size

What do you think you will find if you measure and compare the head circumference of ten adults and ten children?

You will need to use a flexible (plastic or paper) measuring tape around the part of the head just above the eyebrows. Plan how to record your results. (You may need to take measurements to the nearest centimetre to make it easier to record your results.)

When you plot the results on a bar chart what do you notice?

Why did you need to take such a big sample of people?

Mending bones

Bones are strong, but they can break. It can be very painful when a bone breaks, but bones can mend themselves because they are partly made up of living cells. At the point of damage, the bones will produce lots of new cells and tiny blood vessels to rebuild the bone and close up the break. A doctor usually puts on a splint or a plaster cast that keeps the ends of the broken bone still and together until it mends.

Healthy bodies and bones

Eating a balanced mixture of different kinds of foods is vital for a healthy body and healthy bones. Food gives the body the energy it needs to live and the materials it needs to grow. Eating the right foods helps keep bones healthy. Leaving healthy foods out of a person's diet can even cause the long bones in the arms and legs to stop growing.

Healthy eating

To see what we should eat and what we should avoid, we can use a food pyramid like this one. We should try to eat carbohydrates, such as potatoes, rice and pasta, and fruit and vegetables with every meal. Foods rich in protein help to build healthy body parts. We need some foods from the top group, the fats and sugars, but we should only eat small amounts of these.

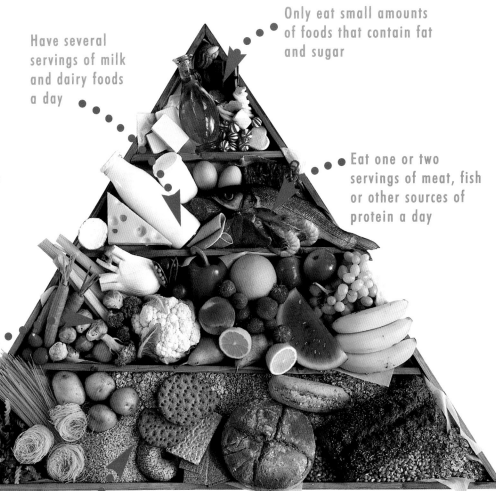

▼ *A balanced diet should include some foods from each of the food groups in the food pyramid.*

Only eat small amounts of foods that contain fat and sugar

Have several servings of milk and dairy foods a day

Eat one or two servings of meat, fish or other sources of protein a day

Eat at least five portions of fruit and vegetables a day

Eat bread, other cereals or potatoes with every meal

Building bones

Bone is mostly made of calcium. Calcium helps to harden and strengthen existing bones, and it helps new bone growth. The human body cannot make calcium so we have to take in calcium in our food. Foods that contain calcium include dairy products (such as milk and cheese), green leafy vegetables (such as spinach), beans, nuts and seeds. Fish with bones that are soft enough to eat, such as sardines, are also rich in calcium. Why do you think this is?

▲ Drinking milk or eating cheese or yogurt is a good way to build stronger bones. Which calcium-rich foods and drinks do you eat every day?

Weak bones

The skeleton grows gradually stronger and denser from childhood until a person is in their thirties. After this, bones lose an average of 1 per cent of their density every ten years as they naturally lose some calcium. Bones become thinner and weaker and break more easily. Women face an extra problem, because in their fifties they lose around 1 per cent of bone density every year for several years. It is very important to build strong bones when we are young, because it will help to slow down the process of bone weakening as we get older.

Play the maze game

Find out how much you really know about growing up with healthy bones at http://www.bonezone.org.uk/ growingup.asp

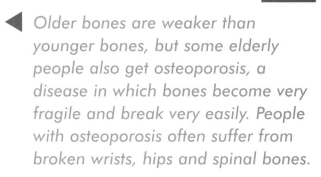

◄ Older bones are weaker than younger bones, but some elderly people also get osteoporosis, a disease in which bones become very fragile and break very easily. People with osteoporosis often suffer from broken wrists, hips and spinal bones.

Exercise

We all need regular exercise to keep fit and healthy but also to keep bones and muscles working well. Exercise makes our muscles and bones bigger and stronger. If you have ever spent a few days in bed because you were unwell, you may have felt weak and a bit wobbly when you got up. That was partly because of the illness, but it was also because you had not been doing any exercise.

Exercise and bones

If we do not exercise regularly our bones and joints may get stiff and then they may not move so well. That is when our bodies become less supple and do not bend so easily. It is important to do a variety of different activities to exercise all parts of the skeleton. Activities such as dancing, playing tennis, gymnastics and even walking keep bones strong. We can also do some gentle stretching and bending exercises on the floor at home to help keep our joints flexible.

Muscles

How do you feel after exercise? Do you feel tired, warm and puffed out? We feel puffed out because the heart is pumping oxygen and blood to the

▲ *How many different forms of protection is this skateboarder wearing?*

Taking care

To protect your bones, take proper precautions if you are doing an activity such as biking, skateboarding or rollerblading. Wear a helmet and some knee and elbow pads to provide extra padding and protection. Accidents may happen, but you can prevent injuries by wearing protective gear.

muscles to help them work and the exercise is making the heart pump faster than normal. The increased blood flow also makes us feel warm. We feel tired because our muscles have had to work harder. But exercise makes our muscles stronger. Strong muscles have more stamina, which means they can keep us moving for longer, and they are less likely to get injured. Different activities exercise different muscles. Walking, running and cycling are good for building strong leg muscles.

Can you think of three kinds of exercise that would be good for the muscles in your arms?

Exercise survey

Do a survey of the amount of time children in your class spend exercising in a week. Record the information using a bar chart on the computer. Label the x-axis with time spans (such as 30 minutes to one hour, one hour to two hours, and so on) and number the y-axis to show how many children fit into each time span.

◀ *Wheelchair athletes develop strong and powerful muscles in their arms and upper bodies to move their wheelchairs fast and over long distances.*

Plan your routine

By eating healthy foods and taking exercise we can keep our bodies strong and healthy. By eating sensibly, we can help our bodies grow, and protect against future illness. Why not improve your health by planning a week's healthy meals and keeping a diary to find out how much exercise you do?

Meal planner

When you plan a week's meals, think about the food pyramid and try to include a variety of different foods of the right amount. When we eat, the body converts nutrients in food to energy, which we use for everything we do. Calories are a measure of how much energy a food supplies us with. The calories that the body does not use up in exercising are stored as fat. People need to choose a calorie intake that matches the amount of exercise they do.

Exercise diary

Keep a diary to note down the amount and type of exercise you do over a week or over a fortnight.

Include the time you spend doing activities such as cycling to school or playing football at break-time. Type up your diary on a computer. When you print out your exercise diary what do you find?

Make a list of other activities you would like to try. We should all try to do half an hour to an hour's activity every day to be fit. Doing more is fine, but it's important not to overdo it.

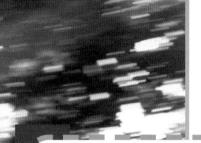

◀ The key to getting enough exercise is to choose something that you enjoy and to do a variety of different activities.

Pulse rate

Your pulse rate is how many times your heart beats in one minute. When you are resting your pulse rate is about 70 beats per minute. Pulse rates increase during exercise because the body's cells need more food and oxygen. The heart beats faster to pump more blood to the cells.

Take your pulse rate sitting down, then after running on the spot for three minutes. What's the difference? Take your pulse rate after exercise every day for a week. Do a different activity every day. Which activity makes your heart work hardest? Make a line graph with the result. What will you put on each axis of the graph?

▲ You can feel your pulse rate as a throbbing in your wrist.

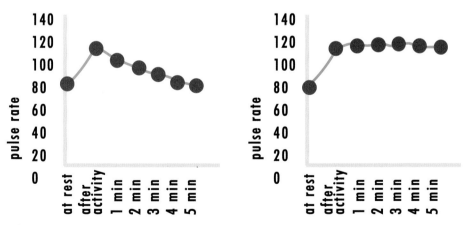

▲ Which one of these line graphs shows what happens to a person's pulse rate when they exercise and then stop to rest, and which is false?

Rest and repair

It's important to exercise, but also to get enough rest and sleep. During the day, the body is busy keeping us on the move. While we sleep, the body repairs the bone cells we need to grow and the muscle cells we need to move.

Glossary

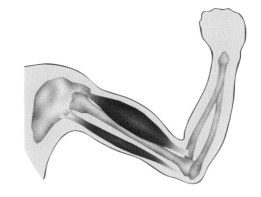

biceps — a large muscle at the front of the upper arm.

calcium — a mineral that the body uses to harden bones.

calorie — the measurement of the energy content of food.

carbohydrate — a type of food that gives the body energy.

cartilage — a smooth, rubbery material that cushions the ends of joints in the body and forms the end of the nose and earlobes.

cell — the smallest part of the body. Every body part is made up of millions of tiny cells.

circumference — the distance around something.

classify — to divide similar things into groups.

contract — to become shorter. Used to describe the way muscles get shorter and pull on bones.

energy — the ability to do work. People get energy from food.

exoskeleton — a hard external layer that provides support and protection for some invertebrates.

fin — the body part that helps fish steer and stay upright in water.

fossil — the remains or trace of a plant or animal that died long ago.

habitat — the place where an animal lives and that provides it with the things it needs, such as food and shelter.

invertebrate — an animal without a spine, such as an insect, worm or crab.

joint — the place where two bones meet inside the body.

ligament — bands of fibre that connect bones with other bones.

limb — a jointed bony body part that animals use for movement, such as an arm, leg, wing or flipper.

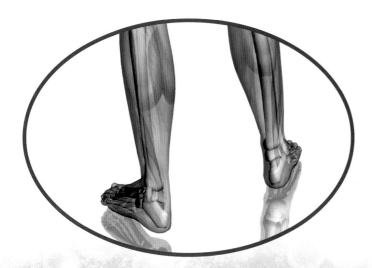

mnemonic	a way of using a pattern of letters to help us remember something.
moult	to shed or lose a skin or exoskeleton to allow an animal's body to grow, or to shed thick body fur or feathers during warmer times of the year.
muscle	a body part that pulls on bones to make animals move.
nerve	a bundle of fibres that carries messages between the brain and the rest of the body.
organ	a body part that carries out a particular job, for example the heart, which pumps blood around the body.
pelvis	the ring of bones to which the leg bones are attached.
predator	an animal that catches and eats other animals for food.
protein	a substance in some foods that the body uses to build or repair body parts.
relax	to make less rigid. Used to describe the way muscles stop pulling and go back to their original length.
reproduce	to have offspring or young.
ribs	the set of long, curved bones that form a protective cage over the heart and lungs.
skeleton	the framework of bones that holds up the body.
skull	the bony structure that protects the brain.
spine	the backbone, formed from a row of linking bones called vertebrae that hold the spine upright.
stamina	having strength and energy that last a long time.
symmetry	identical shapes on both sides.
tendon	a bendy cord that attaches a bone to a muscle.
tissue	a part of the body that has a specific job to do, such as skin, muscle, bone or cartilage.
triceps	a muscle on the back of the upper arms that straightens your elbows and allows you to push your arms forward.
vertebra	(plural vertebrae) one of the bones that make up the spine.
vertebrate	an animal with a spine, such as a cat, human or owl.

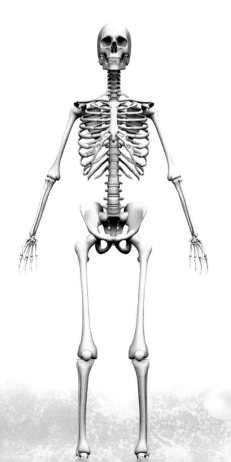

For teachers and parents

This book is designed to support and extend the learning objectives for Unit 4A of the QCA Science Schemes of Work.

Children are naturally curious about their bodies and in this unit they learn about how the skeleton protects, supports and moves humans and what happens to the skeleton and muscles as they move. This understanding is deepened by comparisons of human bones with skeletons of other animals. It also encourages children to relate an understanding of science to their personal health.

Throughout this book and throughout their own investigative work children should be aware that science is based on evidence and they should have the opportunity to:

- Turn questions into an investigation.
- Predict results.
- Understand the need to collect sufficient evidence.
- Understand the need to conduct a fair test.
- Choose and use appropriate measuring or investigation equipment.
- Record results using tables and bar charts, sometimes using ICT.
- Interpret evidence by making observations, comparisons and conclusions using scientific language.

There are opportunities for cross-curricular work in literacy, numeracy, art, design technology and ICT.

SUGGESTED FURTHER ACTIVITIES

Pages 4 - 5 Moving and growing
Outline how and why we classify things. Children could collect pictures from the Internet or magazines or draw some themselves to create a display of living and non-living things. You can download a set of cards to classify at http://www.exploringscience.co.uk/about/downloads/orig/s_and_p_act/b1a8.pdf

Children sometimes find it hard to understand that plants can move and be sensitive so this may require explanation. They could do an experiment to see how a plant's leaves gradually react and turn to face the sunlight or watch flowers (such as tulips) at regular intervals to see that some close their petals at night and open them in the day.

Children could find out more about how X-rays work and look at more X-ray images of the human skeleton at http://www.rad.washington.edu/RadAnat/Hand.html

It may be possible to visit an X-ray room at a clinic or hospital.

Pages 6 - 7 A frame of bones
Use a model skeleton for children to familiarise themselves with the bones of the skeleton. Or examine a virtual skeleton at http://www.ehc.com/vbody.asp, a useful programme to run with an interactive whiteboard, especially if your school does not own a model skeleton. Children can construct the skeleton and label it using the diagram on the whiteboard.

Some children think teeth are bones because they are often shown as part of a model skeleton. Explain why this is not so.

At http://www.bbc.co.uk/schools/podsmission children can put a broken skeleton back together again.

Pages 8 - 9 Support and protection
Children could investigate further what some of the major organs do to aid their understanding of the importance of the bones of the skeleton for protection. Using a blank outline of the human body ask them to draw in the bones that protect the brain and the heart and lungs.

Explain how concept or mind maps work and after the children have looked at the one here they could make one of their own, perhaps with illustrations. They could use computer software such as Textease to produce a concept map onscreen, and enhance the map with pictures, sounds and digital photos.

Pages 10 - 11 How bones move
If possible, use a model to demonstrate how muscles move bones and to help children understand how muscles work in pairs.

Using muscles and bones to move legs is not the only way people move. Children could find out about how paralympic athletes move in wheelchairs using their arms to power themselves along. Or look at the kinds of transport people use, from those powered by muscles and bones (bicycles) to forms of transport powered by fuel.

Pages 12 - 13 Joints and bones
Children could examine the movement of the joints using chicken leg bones. Introduce the term 'articulation' and link to articulated lorries. Ask children to explain in their own words the different types of movement allowed by different joints.

Some joints in the body, such as those in the skull, are fixed and don't allow any movement. Some children may have babies in the family and be interested in the fact that a new baby's skull bones are not joined together (hence the fontanelle, or soft spot), but that the bones quickly grow together to protect the brain.

Research how joint disease occurs and how technology is used to repair damaged joints, such as the hip and knee joints.

Pages 14 - 15 Animal skeletons

Children should be able to examine some sterilised bird, fish or other animal bones to feel how light they are. They could work out where each bone might have been in the animal's body. As they look at real or online skeletons, encourage them to think about questions such as 'Do animals have ribs too?' and 'What parts of the skeleton of this animal are similar to a human skeleton?' They could break open the bones and view them under a magnifying lens.

This is a good time to link with PSHE to discuss the fragility of the animal bones they are holding and why that shows we should be gentle with animals, because their bones can break easily.

Children interested in dinosaurs and extinct animals could go on a trip to a local museum and see dinosaur and other skeletons. (Make sure any off-site visits are carried out in accordance with LEA/school guidelines.) Oxford University Museum has hundreds of animal skeletons and they have several excellent online resources, including http://www.oum.ox.ac.uk/educate/resource/aniskel.pdf and http://www.oum.ox.ac.uk/learning/pdfs/dinosaur.pdf

Make an art attack 'attackosaurus' dinosaur fossil following instructions at http://www.hitentertainment.com/artattack/attackosaurus.html

Pages 16 - 17 Animals without bones

Ask the children to research information about two or three invertebrates and write and draw about how their bodies are supported without internal skeletons.

Children could also find out how many times a shelled or armoured invertebrate sheds its exoskeleton. Discuss why the animal would be vulnerable until its new shell hardens and tactics the animal might have for protecting itself at that time.

Invertebrates can be collected from a variety of habitats, such as leaf litter, grass, trees and bushes, and ponds. Children could collect and observe some invertebrates from a local habitat and identify them using pictorial identification sheets and keys.

Pages 18 - 19 How do animals move?

Children could listen to or compose music that suggests different kinds of animal movement, such as the marching of elephants and slithering of Kaa, the snake, in Disney's early *Jungle Book* film.

Pages 20 - 21 Growth

Discuss what it means to be grown up, or reach maturity. In the case of the animals, it means the point at which they are able to reproduce and stop growing. Note that plants do not stop growing; they grow throughout their lives. Discuss what age people reach adulthood and what puberty means.

When the children do their bar charts, encourage them to talk about what the bar charts show and to think about why charts and tables are useful ways of presenting and analysing information.

Pages 22 - 23 Healthy bodies and bones

Children can find out more about broken bones at http://www.kidshealth.org/kid/ill_injure/aches/broken_bones.html. This site explains what happens when a bone breaks and how doctors help it to heal.

Children could look at and discuss the causes and cures of common sports injuries, including those they or their friends or family might have experienced.

The British Nutrition Foundation site http://www.foodafactoflife.org.uk/ has lots of support and downloadable resources for teachers about healthier eating in school.

Pages 24 - 25 Exercise

Being weightless in space might sound like fun but children might be interested to know that it causes muscles and bones to weaken (and even causes bone loss) because in space astronauts' limbs no longer have to bear the skeletal weight they do every day on Earth. This is why astronauts have to do special exercises in space. See http://exploration.nasa.gov/articles/issphysiology.html for more information.

Pages 26 - 27 Plan your routine

Children could make a line graph with labels at the points where pulse rates were taken to say what activity they were doing at that point. They could use a spreadsheet to record pulse readings from a class using a downloadable spreadsheet from http://curriculum.becta.org.uk/docserver.php?docid=1433

As part of planning a healthy new routine, children could discuss ways of cycling or walking to school, if safe, instead of being driven.

Index